This Book Belongs To:

_____

Statue of Liberty

Empire State Building

Brooklyn Bridge

Times Square

Central Park

One World Trade Center

Metropolitan Museum of Art

Rockefeller Center

Grand Central Terminal

Chrysler Building

The High Line

The Flatiron Building

St. Patrick's Cathedral

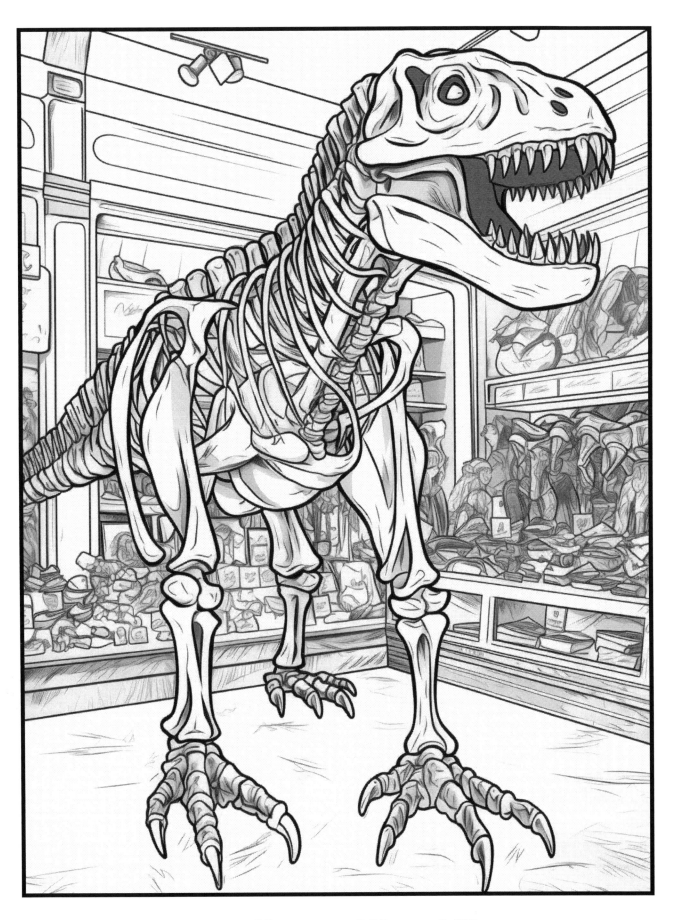

American Museum of Natural History

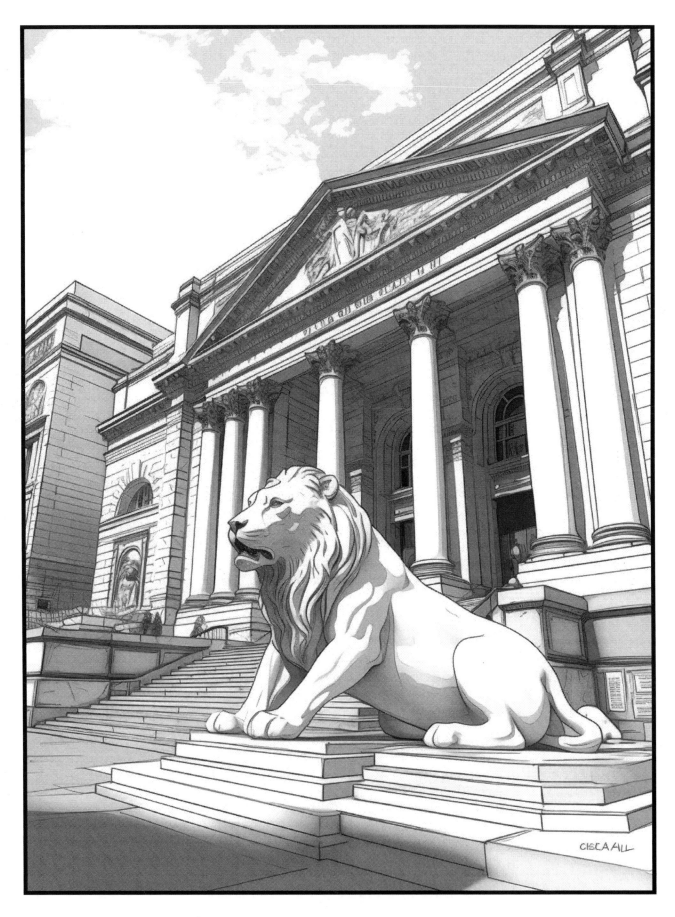

The New York Public Library

Brooklyn Heights Promenade

Wall Street

Washington Square Park Arch

NYC Subway

Madison Square Garden

Soho

NY Stock Exchange

Staten Island Ferry

World's Fair Unisphere

Coney Island Cyclone

WE VALUE YOUR FEEDBACK

Thank you for your journey through our coloring book! If you enjoyed your experience with this book, please consider leaving us a review.

By leaving a review on Amazon:

1. **You Guide Others:** Your honest feedback helps future customers make informed decisions about our book.
2. **You Help Us Improve**: Your constructive criticism guides us in refining future editions
3. **Get The Word Out:** You help others find this book and trust that it is quality content.

Scan the QR code below to share your thoughts:

Thank you for your support!
-Color The City

Printed in Great Britain
by Amazon

37380854R00031